The Questions Dictionary of

Religious Education

Dr Elizabeth Ashton

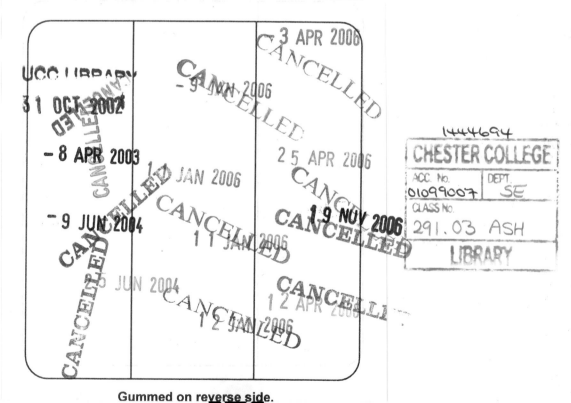
QUESTIONS
PUBLISHING

THE *QUESTIONS* PUBLISHING COMPANY LTD
BIRMINGHAM
2002

The Questions Publishing Company Ltd
321 Bradford Street, Digbeth, Birmingham, B5 6ET

First published in 2002

ISBN: 1-84190-034-6

Illustrations by Michael Rees
Cover design by Andrew Cottle

Printed in the UK

Also available from Questions Publishing Limited:
The Questions Dictionary of Science
by J. J. Wellington
ISBN: 1-898149-84-4

The Questions Dictionary of Geography and Environment
by Professor Joy Palmer
ISBN: 1-84190-031-1

The Questions Dictionary of History
by Professor Joy Palmer
ISBN: 1-84190-047-8

The Questions Dictionary of Art
by Rob Barnes
ISBN: 1-84190-034-6

The Questions Dictionary of Music
by Karen Thornton
ISBN: 1-898149-85-2

ABOUT THE AUTHOR

Dr Elizabeth Ashton taught in primary school classrooms for many years before becoming Lecturer in Religious and Moral Education at the University of Durham. She is author of *Celebrating Our Environment* (1993) and *Religious Education in the Early Years* (2000) and has co-authored books with Dr. Brenda Watson. She has been published widely in both academic and professional journals and is an experienced external examiner in courses of Initial Teacher Training and Higher Degrees in education.

INTRODUCTION

The key words of religion are exciting. They help understanding move beyond the daily concerns of everyday life towards thoughts and ideas which probe the possible meaning and purpose of life and its values. Because of the complexity of the ideas and concepts these key words attempt to express, they can cause difficulties to the student near the beginning of what can be a lifetime's exploration of religious insights and wisdom.

This dictionary is both a guide for the explorer and a mine of information for the reader who is curious to learn more concerning the fundamental concepts of the great religions of the world and the vocabulary in which they are expressed. It should be invaluable for motivating a deeper interest and for stimulating enthusiasm for making fuller investigations into the questions which people continually ask about life's meaning and purpose, and how the positive values which we all have the potential to hold can grow creatively and with responsibility.

USING THE DICTIONARY

Conceptual development lies at the heart of this book. The entries should be looked upon as materials for lessons, rather than simple definitions! There are two important elements to the teaching of religion, and if both are taught, the problem of relativism will have been guarded against. These elements are:

1) understanding and knowledge;
2) helping pupils test the validity of the material against personal experience.

It is all too easy to omit (2) in order to avoid social conditioning, and yet to encourage pupils to test insights in this way is to introduce them to human wisdom which has been found to be supporting and stimulating throughout many millennia.

For example, if 'God' is taught to be a loving father (the metaphor of God's fatherhood), without the introduction of other metaphors (God as energy, a shepherd, light) to give support and to correct misunderstandings, pupils are likely to be left with crude anthropomorphic concepts – that God is an old man in the skies. The idea of God's relationship being like that of a loving father with his children will be lost amongst irrelevancies.

The dictionary should be readily available in both the classroom and school library. It is designed to be used by either individuals or a group of children working cooperatively. Its layout enables teachers to photocopy the entries for mounting on A4 size work cards or for use in displays. The illustrations will appeal to both adults and children, and help bring the text alive.

It is ideal for language teaching and provides an invaluable resource for the Literacy Hour. It is likely to appeal to both the individual who enjoys 'dipping into' books for sheer pleasure, as well as the student seeking specific information.

CLASSIFICATIONS

To help the reader assimilate what might be unfamiliar, and difficult, new words and concepts, the entries have been classified according to four symbols:

   People and Places

 Signs, Symbols and Word Pictures in Religion

Worship and Traditions in Religion

Seasons and Festivals in Religion

PARENTS AND WORK AT HOME

Parents who are keen to encourage the interest of their children in religious ideas and the values which develop from them are likely to find the dictionary:

* ❖ useful and refreshing to their own knowledge about religion;
* ❖ invaluable in that it explains terms drawn from what could be unfamiliar religions and cultures;
* ❖ a stimulus to finding out more;
* ❖ easy to use;
* ❖ helpful for homework;
* ❖ a challenge to many existing ideas about religion.

Dictionary Entries

Abbey

The buildings of a monastery headed by an abbot. The heyday of monasteries was in the Middle Ages. There are still many people today who follow a life of discipline and communal life devoted to serving God in prayer and work.

Abraham

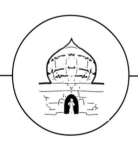

One of the patriarchs of Judaism, who is also prominent in Islam. Stories about him appear in the Hebrew Bible. Believed by some to be a legendary figure, the stories about him in the Bible reflect the ancient world of Mesopotamia and Israel in the nineteenth-sixteenth centuries BCE.

Advent

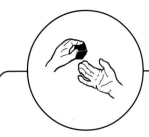

The word means 'the coming', and is the time when Christians, in the four weeks before Christmas, reflect on the meaning of the coming of Christ into the world.

Aidan (Saint)

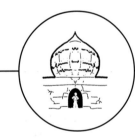

Bishop of Lindisfarne, in Northumberland, died 651 CE. (Saint) Aidan made many journeys on foot in order to make contact with people and teach them about Jesus Christ. He was responsible for establishing the monastery on the Holy Island of Lindisfarne, off the Northumberland coast. His gentleness and sympathy made him loved by the people whom he worked among.

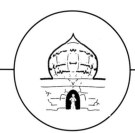

Aisle

The name given to the main corridor in a Christian church, between the rows of pews, which connects the nave with the chancel.

Allah

The name used by Muslims to denote 'God', the creator of the world who revealed himself to Muhammad. Muslims often say, "There is no god but Allah and Muhammad is his prophet".

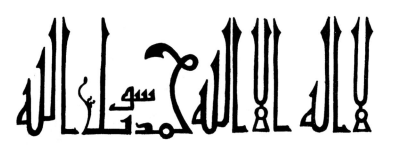

Altar

Table at which, in ancient religions, sacrifices were made. In some Christian churches it is the place where the Eucharist is celebrated.

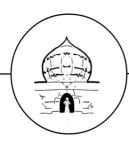

Amritsa

The Holy City of Sikhism, in India. The Golden Temple of Amritsa is encircled by a lake. Hymns in praise of God are sung in the Temple from morning to night. The Temple was built by Arjan, the fifth Guru, at the end of the sixteenth century AD.

Angel

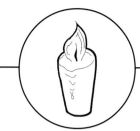

A symbol, especially important in Judaism, Christianity and Islam, which is used in both art and writing to show a person is receiving messages directly from God. In the Greek language 'angel' comes from the word 'to send'. Some people believe angels have a physical existence but many religious people see them as a symbol of spiritual vision, or insight. Symbols are needed because it is impossible to talk about visions and insights in ordinary words, as experiences like these go beyond language. The symbols and signs point towards what is being described.

Apocrypha

Religious writings, both Jewish and Christian, which were not included in the Bible. The word comes from the word 'hidden'. The Jewish Apocrypha is now included in some versions of the Bible, but the New Testament Apocrypha is less common.

Aquinas, Thomas

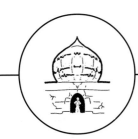

A thirteenth century (AD) Saint, who was very important for the work he did on Christian doctrines, or teachings. The work of Thomas Aquinas was central to the beliefs of the Roman Catholic Church throughout the Middle Ages. He was one of the greatest Christian philosophers and theologians. He was a friar whose work in the thirteenth century is still studied and discussed by thinkers today.

Arabic

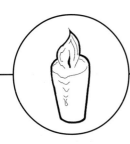

The language in which Muslim Scriptures, the Qur'an was originally written. Islamic children often learn to recite the Qur'an in Arabic, both because of the beauty of the language and also because Muslims believe no translation can carry the original meaning adequately.

Ark

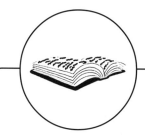

The boat which, as described in the Jewish Scriptures, was built by Noah and his family, as instructed by God. The search for the true ark continues! Stories similar to that of Noah's Ark appear in over seventy cultures of the world, which points to the likelihood of them describing a real event, a real Flood.

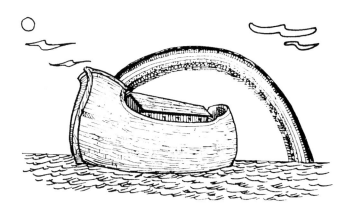

Atman

A word from the Hindu religion which means 'soul', or 'self'. In the Upanishads, Scriptures in Hinduism, the atman is said to be identical to Brahman, or God: the soul is at one with the divine, or holy.

Atonement

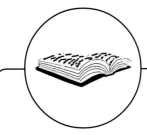

A doctrine, or teaching, in Christianity which accounts for Jesus' death by crucifixion on Good Friday by pointing towards that event and showing how, despite sin and wickedness, people can be 'at one' with God. Using the ancient symbolism of sacrifice, Christianity came to see Jesus' death as the last sacrifice for sin ever needed.

Augustine (Saint)

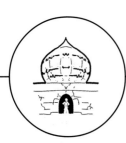

A Christian monk who arrived in Kent, England, in 597 AD to teach the Angles and Saxons – who had invaded after the Romans – about Christianity. Augustine was the first Archbishop in England and founded several monasteries, perhaps the most famous being in Canterbury, which was very important in spreading the teachings of Jesus Christ among the Anglo-Saxon people.

Baptism

The sacrament of entry into the Christian Church. Water stands for washing, cleansing, purifying. Therefore by the use of water, it is shown that the person concerned has become a follower of Jesus Christ and has turned away from evil.

Baptist Church

People who attend the Baptist Church believe in the baptism of adult believers, rather than baptising infants. In the Baptist Church, the person being baptised is totally immersed in water, rather than having water sprinkled over his/her head, as happens in, for example, the Church of England ceremony.

Bar Mitzvah

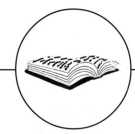

This means 'Son of the Commandment'. This is a 'coming of age' ceremony in Judaism by which boys of thirteen accept the commandments of their faith, and are included in the adult community.

Beautiful Names of Allah

Allah (the name of God in Islam) has ninety-nine names which are known, such as The Merciful, The Loving. No name can describe Allah properly: it is said that the hundredth name of Allah is known only to the camel, which will not reveal its secret! Muslims believe it is impossible to describe Allah so they like to use a lot of names to refer to Him.

Being

Sometimes God is said to be 'being'. This means both that God exists, or that God is real, rather than 'not being', or not existing. It also means that God is the source of being in general – the reason for the universe and for human beings existing. Therefore, to say 'God is being' is similar to saying 'God is real', not made up in the imagination.

Belief

A belief is what is held to be true even if it cannot be proven. Beliefs are held because of the evidence people find for holding them. For example, many people argue for God's existence because there is good in the world, rather than only evil. Many people today think beliefs are subjective: they exist only in human minds, or are what I or someone else happens to think. But reasons can and should be given for beliefs and evidence discussed. It is very important that we should only believe what is true, not what is false or imagination. Beliefs can be very powerful.

Benares

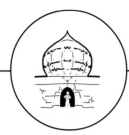

Benares is the most holy city in Hinduism. It is on the banks of the River Ganges, in India, and is a centre for the worship of Shiva. It is visited by at least one million pilgrims each year. The Buddha preached his first sermon here, probably in the deer park on the edge of the city.

Benedict (Saint)

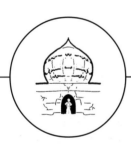

A Christian monk, who lived between the fifth and sixth centuries AD, and is regarded as one of the wisest people in the history of Europe. His Rule, or instructions on how monasteries were to be run, is still followed to this day. The Rule is very down-to-earth and practical. It was balanced, and divided the day into worship and study.

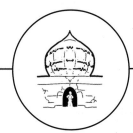

Bethlehem

The town where Jesus of Nazareth was born. Pilgrims can see The Church of the Nativity there, where Christians have worshipped for centuries, and which is traditionally the exact place where Jesus was born.

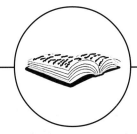

Bhagavad Gita

These words mean 'Song of the Lord', writings that are part of the Scriptures of Hinduism. Part of the writings are a conversation between the warrior Prince Arjuna and the god Krishna, who is disguised as his charioteer. Krishna gives Arjuna encouragement and helps him become wise for the forthcoming battle with the forces of evil.

Bhajana

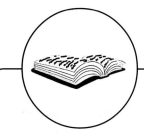

An Indian religious song or hymn in praise of God. It is usually sung with others, rather than alone, during worship, and accompanied by musical instruments.

Bible

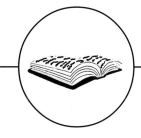

The Bible in Christianity refers to the Hebrew Scriptures (called the Old Testament by Christians) and the New Testament which relates to the impact of Jesus of Nazareth whom Christians believe to be the Jewish Messiah or Christ. The Bible is really a library, rather than one book. There are thirty-nine books in the Hebrew Scriptures and twenty-seven in the New Testament. The first four books of the New Testament tell of the life of Jesus of Nazareth and are called the Gospels (Good News).

Bishop

The most senior priests in some Christian Churches, for example the Roman Catholic Church and the Church of England. Bishops wear special robes, including a specially-shaped hat (a mitre), and they carry a long staff, rather like a shepherd's crook (a crozier). Many Nonconformist Churches do not have bishops.

Brahman

In Hinduism, Brahman is the word given to the Divine, or the Most Holy – the true Reality. All other Hindu gods – with a small 'g' – are thought of as being parts of Brahman, or manifestations. Brahman is considered to be the spirit and heart of the universe.

Buddha (see also Siddhartha)

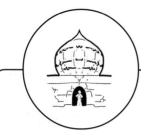

The Enlightened One': the Founder of Buddhism, who was born a Prince in India, in the sixth century BCE. His father tried to hide from him all the unpleasant things in life, but he set out on a spiritual journey to find the true meaning of life. His teachings have had, and continue to have, a profound influence throughout the world.

Caste system

The division of people, within the Hindu tradition, into social groups. In Indian tradition, there are four main groups: Brahmins, the priests; warriors; peasants; unskilled labourers. The untouchables were of no particular caste and could be banished from society. It resembles apartheid, as there are strict rules which forbid ordinary social friendships and relationships between castes. Gandhi sought to abolish the system, but it still survives.

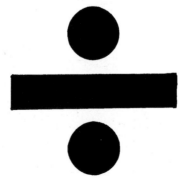

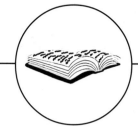

Catechism

Instruction in the Christian faith which gives questions and answers. People getting ready for confirmation are sometimes required to memorize the catechism, although this kind of teaching is used much less now than it was in the past.

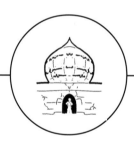

Cathedral

The name given to the large church where a bishop has his throne. The word comes from the Latin 'cathedra', which means 'the seat'. Some cathedrals might be called abbeys if, in the past, the church was part of a monastery – for example, at Durham.

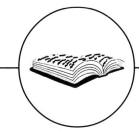

Catholic

Catholic means either (1) 'world-wide', or 'around the world', or (2) a member of the Roman Catholic Church.

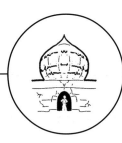

Chancel

In a traditionally built Christian church, the chancel is the part of the church at the east end of the nave, where the choir stalls and the altar were placed where the Mass or Holy Communion was held. This layout is often used today.

Chapel

1) A Christian place of worship, often attached to large houses or cathedrals. (2) A place of worship for people who belong to Nonconformist Churches, for example the Methodists or Baptists.

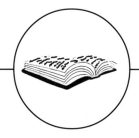

Choir

A trained group of singers who lead the singing in Christian worship, who are often specially trained. Members of the choir may wear robes, for example a black or red gown beneath a white surplice.

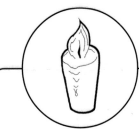

Christ

The special title given to Jesus of Nazareth by the Christian Church. It is the Greek word for 'Messiah', which means 'the anointed one of God'.

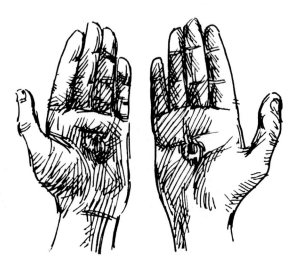

Christianity

The religion which is based on the teachings of Jesus of Nazareth, his life, death and resurrection. The teachings are to be found in the first four books of the New Testament of the Bible (the Gospels), together with accounts of Jesus' birth, life, crucifixion, death and resurrection.

Christmas

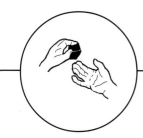

The festival of the birth of Jesus Christ. It is held each year on 25th December, although there is no evidence that Jesus was actually born then. It is possible that Christmas replaced the Roman festival of the birth of Sol Invictus in the fourth century AD.

Church

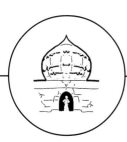

(1) The name often given to a Christian place of worship – but see 'cathedral' and 'chapel', also. (2) A name given to Christian believers, 'the body of Christ'. (3) A local group of Christian believers.

Creation

The act of God which caused the making of the universe. In Judaism, Christianity and Islam the creation is usually thought to have come from nothing. In Hinduism, it is believed that the universe poured from God and will return there at the end of time.

Crucifixion

Death by being nailed on a cross. Crucifixion was a common way of executing criminals in the Roman Empire, and was the method used to execute Jesus of Nazareth. The site of Jesus' crucifixion was Golgotha, outside the walled city of Jerusalem.

Devil

The term used to describe the spirit of evil, or bad. In Christianity, evil is sometimes shown in the person, or symbol, of Satan, who tempts God's people to do wrong.

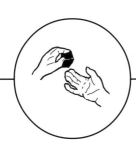

Diwali (Divali)

The Festival of Lights in Hinduism and Sikhism. It is believed, in Hinduism, that the goddess of good fortune, Lakshmi, will visit homes which are lit with lamps, bringing with her good fortune for the coming year. The story of Rama and Sita is retold, and the return of Rama from the forest is celebrated. Sikhs celebrate the release from prison of the sixth Guru. Held in October or November.

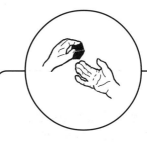

Easter

The Christian festival which celebrates the resurrection from the dead of Jesus of Nazareth. Held March/April.

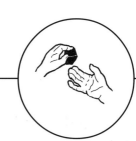

Eid el-Adha

The joyful festival celebrated by Muslims throughout the world, which coincides with the end of the pilgrimage to Mecca. Animal sacrifices are made and the meat distributed to the poor. It celebrates the obedience of Ibrahim (Abraham) in being prepared to sacrifice his son Ishmael (Isaac) to God. Held in May.

Eid el-Fitr

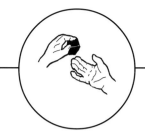

A four-day festival celebrated by Muslims to celebrate the end of Ramadan. Both the poor and children are presented with gifts. Held February/March.

Elohim

The power, or authority, of God. Elohim is a Hebrew word and is used in the great poem celebrating God's creation of the world, which opens the Bible.

Epiphany

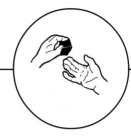

A Christian festival, held on 6th January, which celebrates the coming of the Wise Men to visit the infant Jesus of Nazareth. It also marks 'Twelfth Night', the end of Christmas, when all decorations and cards must be taken down.

Evensong

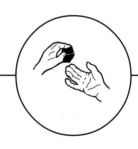

The service of Evening Prayer, held in many Christian churches to give thanks for the past day and to ask for God's protection during the hours of darkness.

Evil

The opposite of 'good', evil has a destructive effect. It can be understood as a force, or power, and is sometimes shown as a person. (See 'Devil'.)

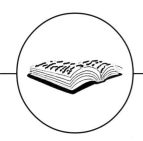

Exodus

The name given to the Flight from Egypt by the Hebrews, who were led by Moses into the wilderness, on the search for the Promised Land. The second book of the Hebrew Scriptures is named after this event.

Faith

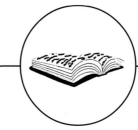

Faith is trust, or commitment, to God or religious teachings. Sometimes the word 'faith' is used to describe beliefs – for example, Roman Catholicism is sometimes called 'the Faith'.

Five Ks (of Sikhism)

The Five Ks are symbols of the Sikh faith. They are:

- ❖ kesh, or uncut hair (a sign of community);
- ❖ kangha, or comb used to keep the hair clean;
- ❖ kara, or metal bangle, which symbolises the belief that God has no beginning and no end;
- ❖ kaccha, or special knee-length underwear which originally allowed free movement in battles;
- ❖ kirpan, or dagger, a symbol of the fight of good against evil.

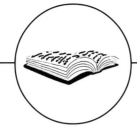

Good Friday

The day when Jesus of Nazareth was crucified on the cross. It is called *Good* Friday rather than *Bad* Friday because Christian doctrine teaches that Jesus' sacrifice sets all those who try to follow God's way in their lives free from evil and promises salvation – they will be saved by God's grace, or power. Held March/April.

Gospel

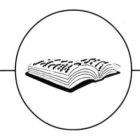

The word 'gospel' means 'good news', and is usually the name given to the first four books of the Christian New Testament: St Matthew, St Mark, St Luke and St John. The 'good news' is about Jesus of Nazareth, his birth, life, teachings, death and resurrection.

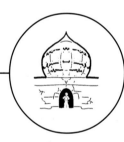

Gregory the Great

Gregory was born in Rome c. 540 AD, and died there 604 AD. (Saint) Gregory was Pope (leader of the Christian Church) at the time when the Roman Empire was breaking up.

In Britain, he is perhaps best remembered for noticing some fair-haired, blue-eyed children in the market place in Rome who were for sale as slaves. On hearing that they were Angles, he said, "They look more like angels". Later, he sent Augustine (subsequently Saint) as a missionary to the kingdom of Kent, where he set up a monastery and began his work of teaching the people about Jesus Christ. He is remembered as being one of the first people to introduce Christianity to the British Isles.

Gurdwara

The Sikh temple and meeting place. At the Gurdwara is to be found a place for worship, and an area for cooking and eating the symbolic meal which takes place at the end of Sikh worship.

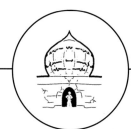

Guru

A word which means 'teacher'. In Indian religion, the title is given to a teacher who helps people understand their own spirituality. In the Sikh religion it is the name given to the first ten teachers who were in charge of the Sikh community.

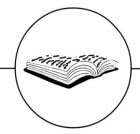

Guru Granth Sahib

The holy Scriptures of the Sikh religion. Many of the prayers included in the Scriptures were written by the founder of Sikhism, Guru Nanak. Great respect is given to the Scriptures, which must be present at the Sikh marriage ceremony. Sikhs consider the Scriptures to be a teacher (guru): hence the name given to the collection.

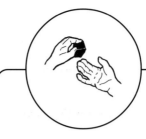

Haaj

In Islam, the Haaj is the pilgrimage to Mecca, and is one of the Five Pillars of Islam. Muslims are expected to make the pilgrimage at least once in their lifetime. Whilst at Mecca, pilgrims touch the Black Stone, the 'Ka'ba'.

Halo

A halo is a often seen in religious pictures (in most of the great world religions). It is a way for the artist to show that the person surrounded by the halo is very close to God.

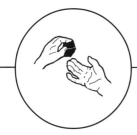

Hanukkah

This is the eight-day festival of Jewish people when they remember the time when the Temple in Jerusalem was recaptured from the Syrians and cleansed, by the orders of the Jewish leader, Judas Maccabeus (died 160 BCE). On each day of the festival one candle in the menorah (branched candlestick) is lit in memory of the rededication of the Temple. Held in December, around the time of the Christian festival of Christmas.

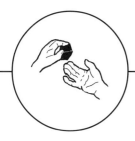

Harvest festival

The Harvest festival is a time when people give thanks for the good things of earth, especially food and drink, which have been safely gathered (harvested). In the Christian Church, the building is often decorated with fruit, flowers and vegetables, and thanks is given to God for the produce. Often, it is taught that people are something like the harvest. Just as there is good and bad fruit, for example, there are good and bad people. God rejoices over the good. Held September/October.

Heaven

Heaven is often thought of as the place of God, (in Christianity especially), but it may also refer to a state of mind, or spiritual development. It is very close to 'nirvana' in the Buddhist faith, a time in human development when wanting the impossible stops. In the Hindu faith, 'moksha' is similar – a time when humans have become freed from the cycle of rebirth.

Hebrews

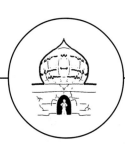

People who were the ancestors of the People of Israel. Their escape from slavery was led by Moses, who led them in the wilderness to find the Promised Land.

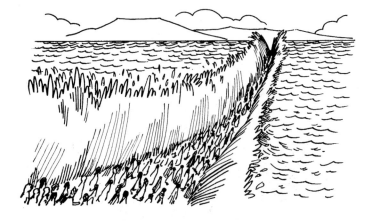

Hindu

A person who follows the ancient religion of India, Hinduism.

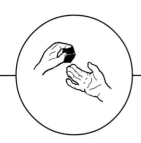

Holi

The springtime festival of Hinduism, which celebrates the beginning of the new planting season. Often, the story of Prince Prahlada and the witch Holika is told, a tale which shows how goodness is stronger than evil. Held March/April.

Holiness

The sacred power of the divine, which is strange and different from ordinary life. The Bible and the Qur'an use the word to describe God. In Christianity, worshippers are called to try to bring holiness into their own lives.

Holocaust

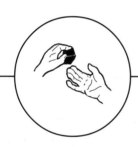

'Holocaust' is a word from the Latin Bible which means 'whole burnt offering'. It is the name given to Hitler's extermination of six million Jewish people in the mid-twentieth century.

Holy communion

The name given by many in the Church of England, and other Protestants, for the service where bread and wine is shared in memory of Jesus of Nazareth's last meal on earth.

Holy Island

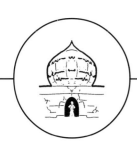

An island off the coast of Northumberland which was important for the establishment of Christianity in England. A monastery there was founded by Saint Aidan.

Holy Spirit

A name often given to God's power. It is used, for example, to describe power which came to the disciples of Jesus of Nazareth on the first Whit Sunday. The power (Holy Spirit) gave the men new courage and strengthened them in their task of spreading the teachings of Jesus of Nazareth.

Hymn

A sacred, or holy song, which is often sung during worship. Hymns are particularly important in Christian and Sikh worship, and in some forms of Hinduism.

Immanent

A word which is often used, for example by Christians, to describe God. It means God is likely to appear at any moment.

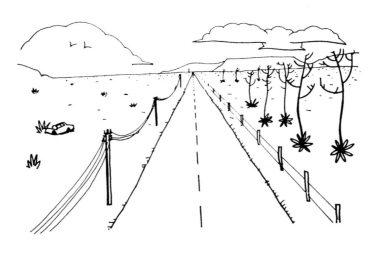

Incarnation

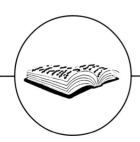

A doctrine, or teaching, within Christianity. It refers to the belief that God became human in the person of Jesus of Nazareth, and is the key to understanding the significance of Christmas.

Isaac

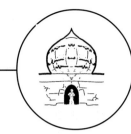

One of the three earliest Hebrew leaders, son of Abraham. The Muslim name for Isaac is Ishmael. In the Jewish and Christian Scriptures is the story of how Abraham was stopped from sacrificing his son Isaac to God by divine intervention – God sent messages to Abraham, who sacrificed a ram instead of his son.

Islam

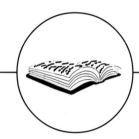

Islam means 'to submit'. This is the name of the religion of Muslims, those who have submitted to the will of Allah. The teachings of Islam are contained in the Qur'an, and comprise revelations to the Holy Prophet Muhammad, whilst he rested in a cave. He asserted the revelations were given him through the Archangel Gabriel.

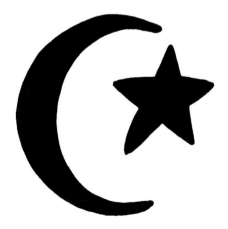

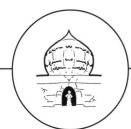

Jacob

Jacob was an early patriach of Judaism, brother of Esau and father of Joseph, who was enslaved in Egypt. The Twelve Tribes of Israel descended from Jacob's Sons.

Jehovah

The sacred name of God, used by the Jewish people. The name means 'I Am'. (See YHWH for more information.)

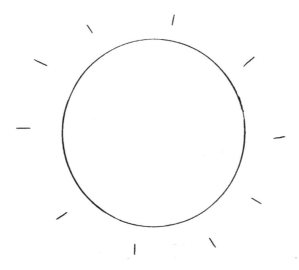

Jerusalem

Jerusalem is the city held sacred by three of the great world religions – Judaism, Christianity and Islam. Jerusalem was a fortified city from ancient times. It was captured by King David in the tenth century BCE, and became the capital and site of the Temple for the Jewish people.

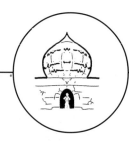

Jesus of Nazareth

The teachings of Jesus of Nazareth provided the basis for Christianity. He was a teacher, leader and prophet, born 4 BCE. Christians believe he was God in human form. Central to the Christian faith is belief that Jesus of Nazareth rose from the dead.

John the Baptist

John was a cousin of Jesus of Nazareth, and lived in wild countryside by the River Jordan and baptised people so they were ready for the coming of the Messiah. Jesus of Nazareth was baptised by him, and received special recognition from God. John the Baptist was beheaded and his head was presented on a silver dish to the King by the dancing girl, Salome.

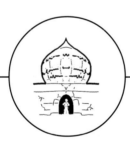

Joseph, father of Jesus

Joseph, the father of Jesus, was a carpenter who lived in Nazareth and was married to Mary. Shortly before the birth of Jesus, Joseph and his wife had to return to Bethlehem, where he had been born, to be registered – the Roman Government had called a census. St. Matthew's Gospel opens with family information which shows how Joseph's family was related to King David of the Old Testament (Jewish Scriptures).

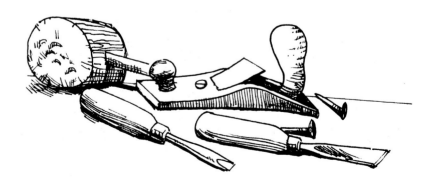

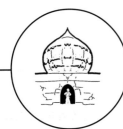

Joseph, son of Jacob

Joseph, Jacob's son, is famous for his coat of many colours, and also for being sold into slavery by his brothers. He eventually reunited his family in Egypt. The story of Joseph is to be found in the Book of Genesis, Christian Old Testament (Jewish Scriptures).

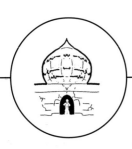

Judas Maccabeus

The leader of the Jews who defeated the Syrians and cleansed and restored the Temple at Jerusalem. He died 160 BCE. (See Hanukkah.)

Judaism

The name of the religion and culture of the Jewish people. Judaism is based on belief in one God, who revealed himself to Moses on Mount Sinai, when the Law (the Torah) was given.

Judgement

In the Old Testament (Jewish Scriptures) God is shown as a judge who will reward or punish people according to their behaviour and standards in life. This idea is central to Christianity, too, but here self-judgement is important also.

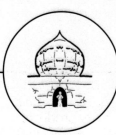

Ka'ba

The Ka'ba is a sanctuary in Mecca. Muslims face Mecca to pray. Set in a corner of the Ka'ba is the Black Stone, which is touched by pilgrims as they file around the sanctuary. The word ka'ba means 'cube'.

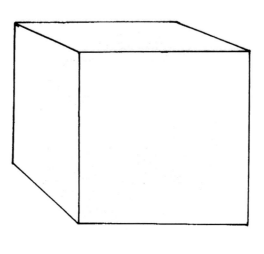

Koran (see Qur'an)

The Koran is the book of Holy Scriptures of Islam. It is usually spelt 'Qur'an'. (See 'Qur'an'.)

Kosher food

Food which is 'clean', according to Jewish law. Meat and dairy products must not be served at the same meal, for example, and pork and shellfish must not be eaten. The Jewish housewife has responsibility for ensuring that the rules concerning diet are kept.

Lent

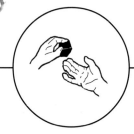

The forty days and nights leading up to the Christian festival of Easter. During Lent, Christian people remember the temptations of Jesus in the wilderness. It is a time when people 'give up' something, or practise self-denial. Many Christian Churches provide Lent boxes, or collecting boxes, into which money which has been saved is placed, and given to good causes.

Light and darkness

Light and darkness are symbols, or signs, which are to be found throughout the great religions of the world. Light symbolises the presence of God and darkness the absence of God. Candles, haloes, and any other form of light, are used as a sign of God.

Lotus flower

The lotus flower is an important symbol of spiritual goodness which is found in the Eastern religious traditions, especially Hinduism and Buddhism. The lotus plant begins life in the muddy waters of the lake, but when it is fully grown it is one of the most beautiful flowers in the world. It is, therefore, used to symbolise how even the poorest person can become spiritually rich.

Lotus position

This is a style of sitting upright, and cross-legged, when meditating. It is used especially by Hindus and Buddhists.

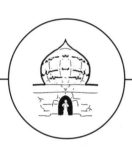

Mandir

The name given to a Hindu temple, or place of worship.

Martyr

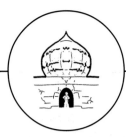

This word means 'witness'. A martyr is someone who died rather than give up a religious faith, especially during persecution.

Mary, mother of Jesus of Nazareth

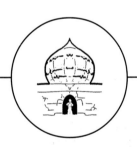

Mary, mother of Jesus, is also called the Virgin Mary, or the Madonna. She is important throughout the life of Jesus of Nazareth, and was one of the women at the foot of the cross during her son's crucifixion.

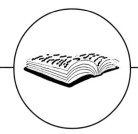

Mass

The name given by Roman Catholic Christians to the Eucharist, or Holy Communion Service. The Mass is centred around the sacrifice of Jesus of Nazareth.

Mattins (matins)

The Christian service of Morning Prayer, held in Church of England cathedrals and churches. Mattins is one of the ancient services of the monasteries.

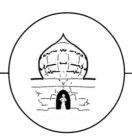

Mecca

The Holy City of Islam, in Saudi Arabia, the birthplace of the prophet Muhammad. Muslims make pilgrimages to Mecca. (See 'Ka'ba'.)

Medina

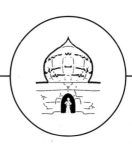

A city north of Mecca, which was a base for the prophet Muhammad before he recaptured Mecca. In Medina is the site of Muhammad's tomb.

Meditation

A way of calming the mind and body by relaxing and thinking hard about some aspect of religion or belief.

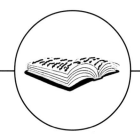

Menorah

A seven-branched candlestick used in Judaism. During the festival of Hanukkah one candle is lit each day until, by the end of the week, the whole menorah is ablaze.

Messiah

'The anointed one'. Messiah is a title often given to Jesus of Nazareth. It means that he was the chosen leader, sent by God to be a leader, or king. It is a Hebrew word.

Metaphor

A metaphor is an idea or insight which is passed on by showing how it is rather like something already known. Metaphors are used throughout religion because often it is impossible to describe the idea or insight in everyday words.

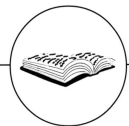

Methodism

Methodism is a branch of the Christian Church. The churches are often called chapels. Methodism developed from the ideas of John and Charles Wesley, who travelled around Britain preaching to people during the eighteenth century.

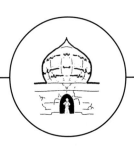

Minster

The name given to a Christian church which once had priests who went out from the church into the countryside to teach the people – for example, York Minster.

Miracle

Something which happens that has been thought impossible. Miracles are thought to be the result of divine, or God's, action.

Moksha

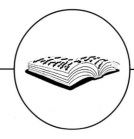

'Freedom': a word which, in Hinduism, means freedom from the round of rebirths, the goal of the Hindu.

Monastery

The place where a community of monks live, or used to live.

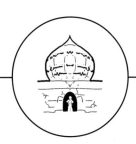

Monk

A man who is a member of a religious community who usually makes vows, including one to obey orders, and who wears clothing called a 'habit'. Monks are to be found in Christianity and Buddhism.

Moses

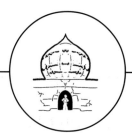

The Father of Judaism, who received the Law (the Torah) from God. He led the Israelite people out of slavery in Egypt to find the Promised Land.

Mosque

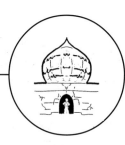

The place of worship of Muslims, which has an outer courtyard for ritual washing and an inner area for worship. Usually the main service is held between noon and 3.00 p.m. on Fridays.

Muezzin

The man who calls the people to prayer from the minaret (tower) of the mosque.

Muhammad (peace be upon him)

Muhammad is the great Prophet of Islam. Born in Mecca, he is believed by Muslims to be the final Great Prophet who summed up the teachings of all the former prophets. He received divine messages from Allah, through the Archangel Gabriel. These later became an important part of the Scriptures of Islam, the Qur'an.

Nanak

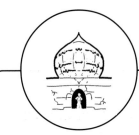

Guru Nanak was the founder of the Sikh religion. He was born in 1469 CE and died in 1539 CE. At first he meant to unite Hindus and Muslims. It is remembered how on his birthday he disappeared into the lake whilst swimming and did not appear until hours later, when his friends thought he had drowned. When he was found to be alive and well, he had thought out what work he believed he had to do to improve the religious life of his society.

Nativity

The name given to the birth of Jesus of Nazareth, especially the story from St. Luke's Gospel which tells of the angels bringing the shepherds the good news and also the account of the birth of Jesus in the stable at Nazareth.

Nave

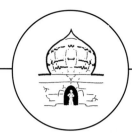

The nave is the name given to the part of the traditionally-built Christian church which, originally, was the responsibility of lay-people, rather than the priest.

Nazareth

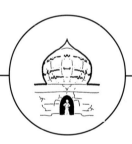

Nazareth is the town in Palestine where Mary and Joseph, parents of Jesus of Nazareth, lived, and where Jesus probably lived as a boy.

Noah

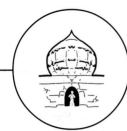

Noah was the man (who can be understood to stand for all good people) who was instructed by God to build an ark to enable the good things of creation to survive the Great Flood. The story of Noah and his family can be read in the book of Genesis (Jewish Scriptures/Christian Old Testament).

Nun

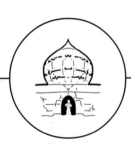

A nun is a woman who makes various religious vows, and usually lives in a convent, a community of nuns who live together. Nuns are to be found in both Christianity and Buddhism.

Parable

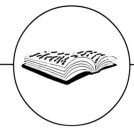

A parable is a story which has a meaning or meanings which go deeper than the obvious, or literal, meaning. Jesus of Nazareth, for example, often used parables in his teachings about the Kingdom of Heaven.

Passover

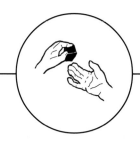

Passover is a seven-day Jewish festival when it is remembered how the Hebrews escaped from slavery in Egypt. Special meals are eaten in Jewish homes, prayers are said and hymns sung as people look to the time when God will rescue, or redeem, them. Held March/April. The festival is also called Pesakh.

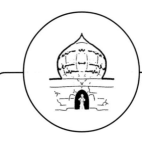

Paul (Saint)

Paul was one of the early, and greatest, of Christian leaders, who is remembered especially as the one who spread the teachings of Jesus of Nazareth throughout much of the Roman Empire. He wrote many epistles (letters) which are in the New Testament. He was a persecutor of the Christians but, after having a vision of Jesus on the road to Damascus, he became a Christian himself.

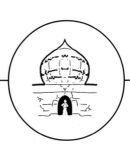

Paulinus

Paulinus travelled with Princess Ethelburga from Kent to Northumbria in 625 CE, when she went to marry King Edwin. Paulinus had come from Rome with Saint Augustine, and was a bishop, responsible for baptising many people into Christianity in England.

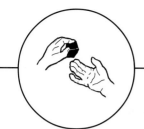

Pesakh

See 'Passover'.

Peter, (Saint)

(Saint) Peter was a disciple, and close friend of Jesus of Nazareth. His real name was 'Simon', but Jesus renamed him 'Peter' which means 'a rock', possibly because in the future Peter was to be especially strong and reliable.

Pilgrim

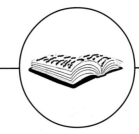

A pilgrim is a person who travels to celebrate a past event, or perhaps to ask for help, at a shrine or holy place. Sometimes prayers may be offered to relics, in the hope that the power of the person whose relics they happen to be will give help in some way – perhaps in curing an illness.

Pope

The Pope is the Bishop of Rome, the leader of the Roman Catholic Christian Church throughout the world. He is taken to be the successor of St. Peter. His authority is not recognised by Protestant Christians.

Prayer

The offering of worship, pleas for help, requests, or quiet meditation, or confession of sin, all in the hope God will respond. Prayers can be offered either privately or publicly, for example, in a church or place of worship.

Presbyterianism

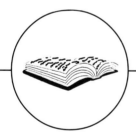

Christian Churches which are based on the ideas of John Calvin (1509-1564 CE). Presbyterianism has been the main Church of Scotland since the early years of the Reformation.

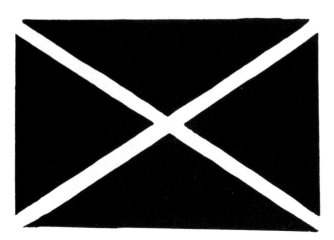

Rig Veda

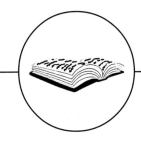

One of the main Scriptures of Hinduism. The Rig Veda is made up of more than one thousand hymns – 'Rig Veda' means 'Songs of Knowledge'. These verses are among the oldest surviving writings in the world.

Roman Catholic

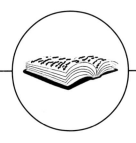

A Roman Catholic is a Christian who recognises the authority of the Pope as the head of the Christian Church (See 'Reformation'.)

Sabbath

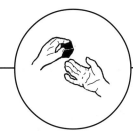

The Jewish day of worship, which lasts from Friday sunset to Saturday sunset. The Sabbath is important as it represents the day of rest taken by God after the six days spent in creating the world. It also reminds Jewish people of their escape from slavery in Egypt.

Sacrifice

A sacrifice is the act of giving up something in order to bring good into an otherwise bad situation. Sacrifices can range from the small (for example, self-denial during Lent or Ramadan) to the large (for example, the Christian belief that Jesus of Nazareth sacrificed his life to defeat death and evil).

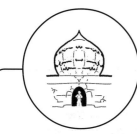

Saint

A holy person, or a dead person who has been held by people on earth to have been especially close to God. Saints are sometimes thought as a channel to God, and their place of burial, or a place where their relics are kept, can become a place of pilgrimage. (See 'Pilgrim'.) Protestant Christians are less enthusiastic about the cult of saints than the Roman Catholic tradition tends to be.

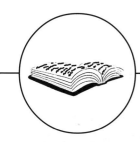

Salvation

Two meanings can be given: (1) In the Bible, 'salvation' can mean the saving power of God, who will rescue believers from evil, death and sin. (2) In Eastern religions, 'salvation' can be from the ordinary, material world to the spiritual.

Salvation Army

A Christian movement which was founded by William Booth in the nineteenth century CE. The movement has been particularly important in bringing the Christian gospel to the poor, or people under stress – for example, soldiers fighting in the two World Wars in Europe. Members wear a uniform, and the movement is well known for its band music.

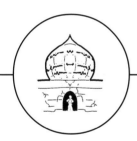

Sanctuary

A sanctuary is a either (1) a safe place, or (2) the most holy part of a Christian Church, often where the altar stands. In earlier times, a sanctuary was a place where criminals were given protection for a short time.

Shiva

One of the great gods of Hinduism. He is the God of opposites, for example good and evil, creation and destruction. He was the first Lord of the Dance who celebrates the creation of the universe.

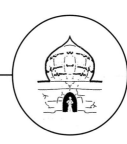

Siddhartha

Siddhartha was the founder of Buddhism (b. 560 BCE). Originally a Prince, he gave up his position and wealth and became a great religious thinker and spiritual leader. (See 'Buddha'.)

Sikhism

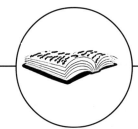

The word means 'disciple', or 'follower'. Sikhism is a religion which developed in India during the sixteenth century CE. Sikhs use the title 'Singh' as a surname – it means 'lion'. (See also 'Nanak', the founder of the religion.)

Sita

A popular Hindu goddess, the wife of Rama. Sita is often shown as the model wife.

Soul

The part of the human which survives the death of the body, as described in most religious writings. In Hinduism, the soul is called 'atman'.

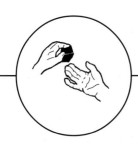

Sukkot

See 'Tabernacles, Feast of'.

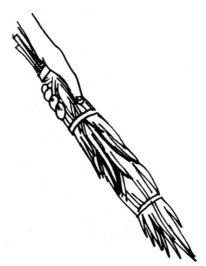

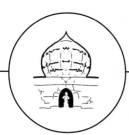

Synagogue

The place of worship of Jewish people. Study is carried out there, too. Synagogues are built to face Jerusalem and contain an 'ark' in which copies of the Jewish law, the 'Torah' are kept. Worship includes psalms, sermons and prayers.

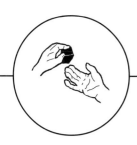

Tabernacles, Feast of

This is a week-long Jewish festival which marks the end of the harvest season. Straw, or branch-covered shelters are often used to remind the people of God's care for the Hebrews after their escape from slavery in Egypt. Held September/October.

Temple of Jerusalem

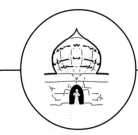

The Jewish Temple in Jerusalem was built in the reign of King Solomon (tenth century BCE). The building was destroyed and rebuilt during several centuries. Its site occupied one quarter of the whole city of Jerusalem. The Temple was the national centre for Jewish worship. Its most holy place was the sanctuary, called the 'Holy of Holies' where the Ark of the Covenant was kept. The Temple was destroyed by the Romans in 70 CE, using fire.

Ten Commandments

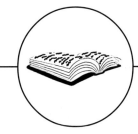

The Jewish Law (the Torah) given by God to Moses on Mount Sinai. The Commandments serve as a foundation of standards for life. They have been of enormous importance for both Jews and Christians, and continue as a sound basis for life in general.

Torah

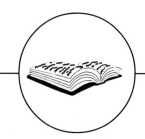

This is the Hebrew word for 'instruction'. This is the word for the Jewish Law, but it is more than that as the Torah also contains divine instructions and revelations from God.

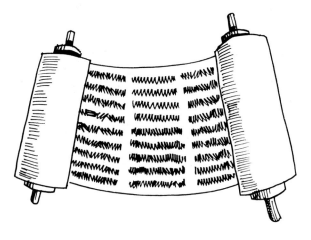

Transcendence

A word often used to describe God. It means God is beyond all that we know, or possibly could know. (See also 'God'.)

Trinity

The Christian teaching that, although there is one God, God is in three aspects, or parts: the Father, Son and Holy Spirit. St Patrick explained the Trinity by showing the people the clover leaf: it had three main parts, but was one leaf. God, he taught, was something like that.

Truth

A word that means 'really is' which is used to describe God. For example, St. John's Gospel explains the truth of God, whilst the Jewish Scriptures (Christian Old Testament) explain 'truth' as God's reliability.

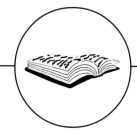

Upanishads

Hindu Scriptures which were written between 800/400 BCE. Understanding of Brahman is explained, and how the soul (atman) is part of Brahman. (See, too, 'Brahman' and 'Atman'.)

Vicar

A priest in charge of a Church of England parish. A vicar lives in a vicarage, a house which may be close to the church building.

Vishnu

In Hinduism, the god of life who gives protection. Vishnu is one of the great gods of Hinduism who is important, for example, in the festivals of Diwali and Holi (see entries for both).

Wesak

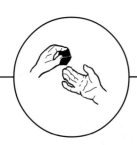

Buddhists celebrate the main three events in the life of the Buddha (Prince Siddhartha): his birth, growth of understanding (enlightenment) and his death, which all happened on the same day of different years. Held in May or June.

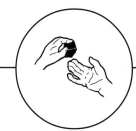

Whitsuntide

The name given to the season when the Christian Church remembers the coming of God's power (Holy Spirit) to the disciples of Jesus of Nazareth. Whit Sunday is sometimes called the birthday of the Christian Church. It is also called Pentecost. Held end of May/early June.

Worship

A way of showing honour to God. Worship varies from one religion to another, but often prayer, singing and chanting are included.

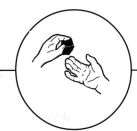

Xmas

A shortened version of the word for the Christian festival of 'Christmas'.

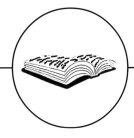

Yoga

A way, in Hindu teaching, to bring oneself closer to God, where deep thought and relaxation (meditation) are important.

Yom Kippur

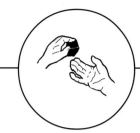

Yom Kippur is the Jewish day of fasting and showing repentance (being sorry) for past wrongdoing. It is the most solemn day of the Jewish year, when a special chant, the Kol Nidre, challenges those who have forgotten about their religious faith to return. Held September or October.

YHWH

The Jewish concept of God. YHWH is never spoken.

Notes

Notes

Notes